THE MATTER OF EXISTENCE

A Collection of Poems

Also by Ciara Attong

Dark & Cold
(Book One of The Dark & Cold Trilogy)

butterfly breaths
A Collection of Poetry

euphorically chaotic dystopias
A Collection of Poetry

Soul Strings
A Collection of Poems

The Hollow Aches
A Collection of Poems

The Matter of Existence

*A Collection of Poems
By Ciara Attong*

The Matter of Existence

© *2023 Ciara Attong*

All Rights Reserved.

All rights reserved in all media. No part of this book may be used or reproduced without written permission, except in the case of brief quotations embodied in critical articles and reviews.

The moral right of Ciara Attong as the author of this work has been asserted by her in accordance with the Copyright, Designs, and Patents Act of 1988.

This is a work of fiction. Any names, persons, places, or objects used in the following are products of the author's imagination, have been used fictitiously or without previous knowledge of existence. Any resemblance to people, places or events is coincidental or fictionalised.

Cultivate.

Evolve, reverently;

For this is the matter of existence.

For Ishwar, Celine, and Cherisse

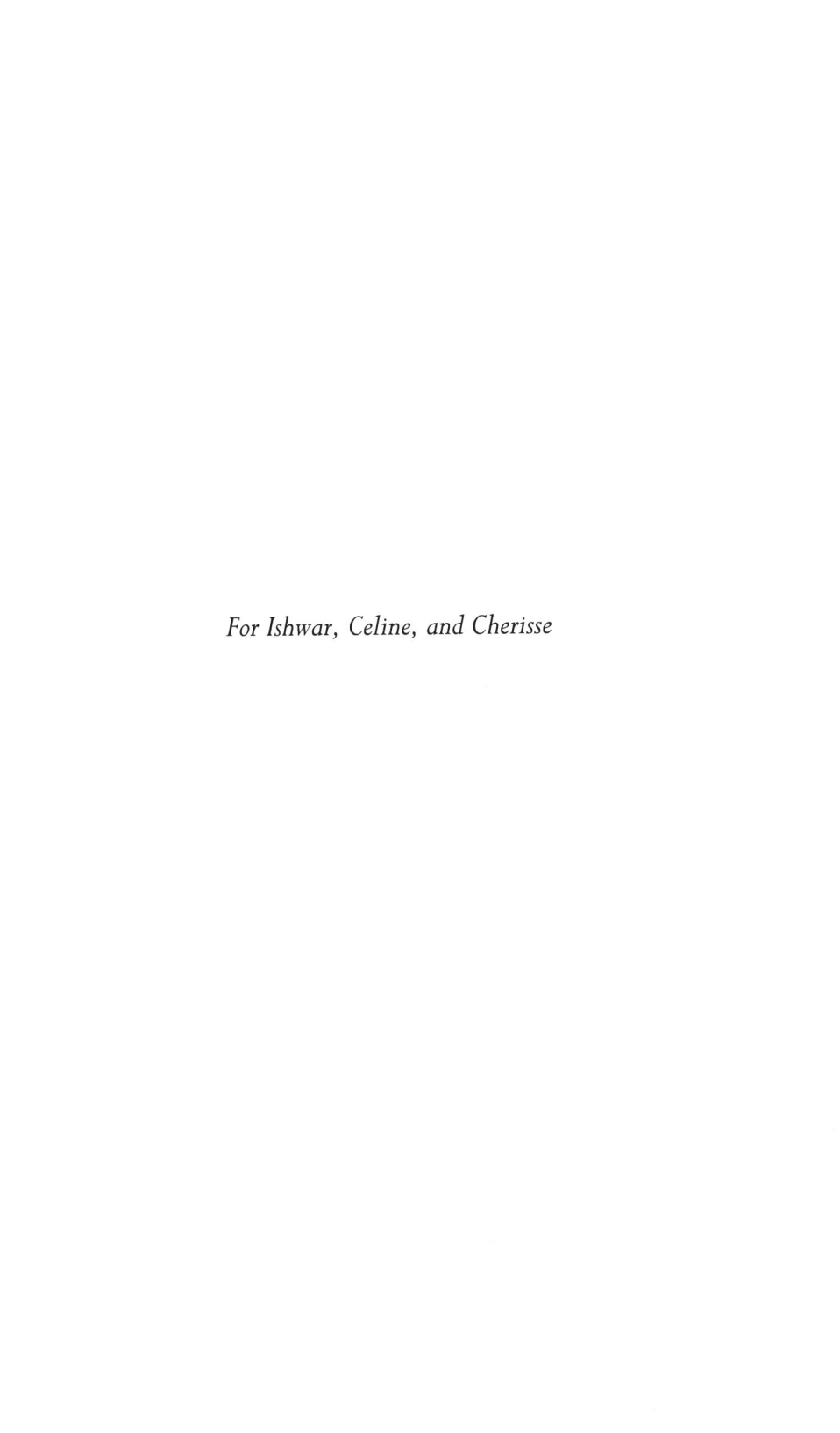

PURPOSE

In the vastness of this undefined plain,
there is nothing -

nothing but Time,

and Change,

and You.

What will you do?

Your purpose is being fulfilled
even right now;
as you breathe,
as you feel.

Don't you know?
That you are an extension -an expansion,
a loud whisper out of the cosmos -
universe-quaking vibrations,
boundless energy -
vibrant passion,
electricity -

Don't you know?
That your voice, your
breath, alone
bounces, echoes - off stars
at the edge of existence?

Don't you know
that you are already all -
a l l the power you will ever need?

Take up space.
Take up space.
Take up space.

.

What is it about
the sky
the rain
the ocean
the waves
the wind
the earth
the heavens
our universe
our heartbeats
all of these things and more
that make us think so deeply?
Is it the thrill and mystery of the unknown?
The desire to dwell in the presence of inexplicable beauty?

Perhaps all of humanity inherently knows it -
that to understand is to expand;
and to expand is to create things anew,
and even if it is unconsciously done,
we are doing exactly what we
were intended to do.

*Purpose and Passion are
both woven
from the same thread.*

Imagine how much deeper
you can understand your own existence -
you can understand
all
of existence -
when you accept that some things
that maybe
all things
are simply
undeniably
inherently intertwined.

You cannot unsee the things
your soul is showing to you

You cannot unhear the whispers

You cannot ignore the signs -

Your destiny is already
written deep within you;
it aches in your bones

with the pungence of purpose,
and the taste of words hesitantly
tipping off your tongue,

whatever fate feels like...

there is no need to search and search
and search

all you have to do
is observe.

Moments;
so short -
so fleeting, yet
so many a times, unforgettable.

Like wind, Life blows by -
and suddenly years are gone.

No two winds sound the same;
they've different voices -
some that whisper, and some that sing
all sorts of different things.

They are as unique as the sunsets
at the end of each day.
So, too, are people,
and the memories they bring.

Fleeting as moments
are all our souls, and these
are the things in life
which we must cherish.

The Monarch will never know
the true potential -the power -
of its wings;

for it simply flies -
and in grace, finds
that all is with the world
as it should be.

Long before we had come to know it,
that great and divine energy that has
eventually come to compose the music of our
heartbeats had been
orchestrating vibrations
beyond our understanding -

Long before we had come to know it,
we were already a part of the greatest symphony -
sweet essence
awaiting our cues in the moving sheets of creation's
ritualistic ceremony.

When I finally awaken,
to my fullest state of enlightenment -
when I open my eyes to behold,
in glorious beauty,
the vastness of the archives
telling the tales of
who I have been,
and who I have become,
and who I am yet to be -

I hope I will look upon
a spirit that has won
all its wars;

I hope I will look upon a soul, so conscious,
it has never been afraid
to evolve.

I am thankful
for the gentle way it was whispered -

it floated towards me
like a soft feather in the wind

as if to say
"all is well"

as if to say...
all that you have experienced;
the tugs of war etched
into history chapters of
your existence -

all of it has prepared you
for this day.

- The Day I Discovered My Purpose

THIS IS YOUR CALL
to worry less about your place in this world
and to focus more
on the things you feel -
on the things you learn -

When you find the feelings,
follow them, within -

They will lead you to the reasons

and they will lead you to the lessons

and eventually,

you will be enlightened

by the purpose.

Feel everything intently;
the great things and the small -
and do not be afraid to ask
the daring questions
of where any of it
is coming from.

PASSION

If, essentially, all I am
is energy,
then it matters not who allows or disallows it;

It is in my design
to vibrate -
to r a d i a t e.

The choice is not
in evolving
for evolving is in our design;

the choice is in the self, discovering
that it can be as simple
or as complex,
as we would like.

Art
is the way
the soul speaks to humanity

The Heart
is the way
humanity responds

Art,
and Heart,
are both soul languages;

Dialects -
used interchangeably
to understand existence.

- *Soul Languages*

There is a level of persistence encompassing the madness
called Passion;
endless echoes of a dream -
sleepless nights when inspiration strikes,
like darts to a bull's-eye -
and lastly,
and most importantly,
there is wildly raging intent,
and there is overwhelming love.

where do my wishes go
when I blow at the florets of a dandelion -
when I close my eyes and meditate
over every 11:11 -
when the shooting stars
cross the skies
just in time for my gleaming eyes -
and I set aside the risk of everything to believe in
them?

do they fly through the wind,
and wither into nothing,
and simply keep cruising across space and time?
or do they maybe
just maybe
find a way to come true?

Cave in
to the tsunamis of imperfection;
for the sooner you free yourself
to drown into it,
the quicker you will find that in actuality
you are floating - rising
above it.

and what colourful mind works with such high zest
as to question that which is mindless
contrary to the mindset of the inquisitive
minds that ponder - inquire, about that which is
carefully considered

Loving
meant realising
I had to use all the love in me
lose all the love in me
so that in darkness - in pain - I could see
that even when I am spent of it all
I am entirely made
of Love.

autumn aches
when you have lost your leaves

mourn delicately

for spring is certain
to come again

- stay rooted

Burning desires
offer us an indescribable feeling of liberation;

as if to say...

> You were designed to be
> an emotional powerhouse;

as if to say...

> You were built
> to act upon and adapt to
> the propelling energy
> of Passion.

SOUL

I imagine an endless existence
where just as a speck of dust
floating through an abandoned hallway,
the matters of the heart

become little to nothing;

become lost in translation -

void of any purpose

of any meaning

and I find myself so grateful
for the opportunity to embrace mortality
to breathe
to experience
to feel
as all the rest of humanity.

Souls are designed
to evolve
throughout a timeless existence;
to expand the universe by expanding itself
in spirit
in heart
in mind -

Souls are designed
with the inherent understanding
that existence is a progressive cycle;

and so we trip through time -
through buds and fruits and withered uproots -
through all of what seems like just
one life

but each time the journey ends,
the soul notes it all
and begins again.

-*Soul Consciousness*

Life is so full of colour -
so full of heart;

In tremendous sorrow and emptiness
would I exist; without a soul that is
open to receiving
any of it.

Love,
my soul,

and so, too, *profoundly* ache —

for in it all is the
testimony

of your strange and notorious journey.

It is the days that you remember most vividly in your
lifetime, that
captain the nurturing your soul,
as it moves forward in its ongoing
evolution.

To be nurtured by the heights and depths of physical existence
is one of the greatest blessings I have;

for my soul cannot feel sunlight,
without a body...

but the sunlight is so good
for my soul.

Wiser than the old
are the ones who recognise
that wisdom is not so much about
how long you have lived
as it is about what you have endured;

Wise are the ones who recognise
that wisdom is a buried treasure
nestled deeply under the rubble
of the hurricanes of change.

Our hearts are broken
and they chip away
little by little,
endlessly
over the course of our lives -

Our souls return
reform
reshape
revitalize
for as long as they must
for all of existence
mending tirelessly -
timelessly.

And why must this cycle happen,
we wonder?
Well darling, I believe,
that a soul is capable of learning;
of growing -
and the heart is its language of comprehension -
there is no way to understand the soul
there is no way to grow in all wholeness and truth
without first feeling
from the heart.

There is spirit left
even in a very dead thing -
for as long as it has once breathed the breath of life,
it carries the weight of a soul.

Mortality is to the soul
as growth is to the seed -

frighteningly uncomfortable and sudden;
frighteningly empowering and necessary.

BREATH

Oh, to be the one -
that one unsuspecting, all-powerful seed;
to break -
to push past all inhibitions...
to grow -
to bloom.

Isn't it refreshing?

The burst of energy —

the adrenaline —

the strength that gathers within you
seemingly out of nowhere?

Do you not believe we are fortunate?
- That the gift of *liveliness* is wrapped
so delicately for us,
every single day?

What a joy it is,
to be alive,
in each passing second that we *are* alive -
awaiting,
anticipating the chances
to unfold it.

- All of Life is Energy

The seasons belong
to us
with us
for us -

nature's reminder, always
that we are, with it, one and the same -
that we are all a part
of a cycle of change -

                              Do we not adapt to it,
                   as though it is "second nature" to us?

Second to nature, is adaptation -

                                              It is.

For every milestone I achieve
as I trickle through Time's sands,
I find myself overwhelmingly grateful for
the stubbornness of my spirit
and the strength of my intuition.

I was given a voice that will
hold the weight of all my words;

a voice that cries out,
bellows -
roars -

a voice that is understood even when
I am caught in trembles -

even when my strength fails
and all I can manage
is a gasp -
a mumble -
a whisper -

My voice holds
unfathomable, irrevocable power;
massive vibrations,
designed to devour.

Someday, when I am gone,
all the art I have created,
all the words I have ever written,
the things I have said to people,
the way I have treated lives around me,
and the work I have done —

I hope I feel contented
in my final moments, knowing
I have left the mark
I wanted to leave
in this lifetime - and that
it was
enough.

Stars die
even as flowers bloom
but we pick the flowers
after joyfully welcoming spring
and we do not mourn the stars;

a sky full of dead stars beckons us to wish -
and plucked flowers -even just petals- pretty the pathways,

doesn't it say
even in death
there is new life given
to everything?

All of life
is energy -

breath;

movement;

Where does it go
when life ends?

some of it transfers
to those around the rippling echo of lifelessness

some goes back to the earth

part of it goes to the creator, perhaps -
the soul -

but even in the loss,
in the death,
in the grief -

understand that energy
never dies.

We do not mourn the seeds
as we grieve others,

burying them into the ground;

for all of life
and all of death

is hope
for what is to come.

Existence,
like a very great song sung from the heart,

will begin with one -
and when they are gone,

will begin with those
who had heard it.

Just as they gathered together
and left the great city behind -
a tower of strength they
were not building for themselves -
Left it marked, unfinished,
Left it,
whole;
with immense clarity —

May you leave this world
with only those
who speak the same language as
your soul.

-B a b e l

Fin

It is all that will be left of us;
ashes, and dust -
and the weight of all
the pieces of our soul
that we have shared
with others.

Author's Note

    This compilation is the fifth poetry collection I have published to date. As I continue to share my works in the form of poetry, I think that after five books, now would at least be a good time to talk a little bit about the intention behind such pieces.

    Each of my collections, inclusive of this one, all represent some kind of *metamorphosis*. Metamorphosis, and as I would call it, *a literary exhibition*, is a compelling call to examine individualistic existence, and to reimagine relationships.

What is your relationship with existence? Do you often contemplate upon the issues of purpose, passion and soul? Do you allow yourself to wholeheartedly feel, and to allow emotions and experiences to open you up to the deeper lessons about life -and about who and what you are?

    Hopefully, this collection gives you a sneak peek into the way the often 'very-subjective' idea of existence plays out in my mind – hopefully, it will open you up to a new way of viewing even the smallest things you might experience.

    I have always opted for making the effort to live my life more intentionally. Have you ever wondered how you can go about doing that for yourself? Well, pondering upon the ideas presented in this collection might just be a great place to start.

About The Author

Ciara Attong is a twenty-three-year-old south-based author, born in Trinidad & Tobago.

She released her first book, a royal teen fiction novel titled "*Dark & Cold*" (the first of a trilogy) in November 2019. She was nineteen years old at the time.

She then went on to publish her first and second poetry books titled '*butterfly breaths*' and '*euphorically chaotic dystopias*' at the beginning of 2022.

In April 2023, Ciara released her fourth book - a poetry collection titled "*Soul Strings*", and in May 2023, she published another collection, titled, '*The Hollow Aches.*'

With her fifth poetry book (and overall *sixth* publication to date) out now, "*The Matter of Existence: A Collection of Poems*" marks a new milestone in the career of the young adult writer.

Ciara enjoys writing works of fiction (novels and novellas) and poetry, and takes an interest in other spheres of creative, visual and performing arts such as in music, acting and visual arts. Aside from being a published author and poet, she is a visual artist who produces original artwork (paintings, illustrations and more) and works by commission.

Attong has no plans to slow down; she is determined to charge headfirst into more experimental creative work. Her goal is to improve and expand in other areas of the creative field where she believes she can maximize her potential, while continuing to do what she does best; creative writing.

Made in the USA
Columbia, SC
25 September 2023